PIONEER GIRL

The Story of
Laura Ingalls Wilder

By William Anderson • Illustrated by Dan Andreasen

HARPERCOLLINS *PUBLISHERS*

Text copyright © 1998 by William T. Anderson • Illustrations copyright © 1998 by Dan Andreasen • Printed in the U.S.A. All rights reserved. • Library of Congress Cataloging-in-Publication Data •
Anderson, William, 1952– • Pioneer girl : the story of Laura Ingalls Wilder / by William Anderson ; illustrations by Dan Andreasen. • p. cm. • Summary: Recounts the life story of the
author of the "Little House" books, from her childhood in Wisconsin to her old age at Rocky Ridge Farm. • ISBN 0-06-027243-0. — ISBN 0-06-027244-9 (lib. bdg.) — ISBN 0-06-446234-X (pbk.)
• 1. Wilder, Laura Ingalls, 1867–1957—Childhood and youth—Juvenile literature. 2. Women authors, American—20th century—Biography—Juvenile literature. 3. Frontier and pioneer life—United
States—Juvenile literature. 4. Pioneer children—United States—Biography—Juvenile literature. [1. Wilder, Laura Ingalls, 1867–1957. 2. Authors, American. 3. Women—Biography. 4. Frontier
and pioneer life.] I. Andreasen, Dan, ill. II. Title. • PS3545.I342Z563 1998 813'.52—dc20 [B] • 96-31203 • CIP AC Typography by Alicia Mikles ❖ Visit us on the World Wide Web!
http://www.harperchildrens.com

L ong ago, in 1867, when America was a land of dense forests and wide, open prairies, a pioneer girl named Laura Ingalls was born. She lived with her Pa and Ma and her older sister, Mary, in a little log house among the big trees of Wisconsin. Laura's earliest memories were of her Pa and Ma packing everything they owned into a covered wagon. In went all their clothes, dishes, bedding, and books, and Pa's fiddle. Laura's family left the little house and traveled for days and weeks. They were going to Kansas.

On a grassy, flat prairie, Pa finally found a spot for a new little house. Log by log, Pa and Ma built the house, and Laura helped Pa build the door. Laura was happy living on the prairie, running in the wind with Jack the bulldog, or exploring in the tall grass with Mary.

An Indian trail curved right through the Ingallses' new farm, and Laura often saw Indians. Although the Ingallses did not know it, they had settled on land that belonged to the Osage Indians. Before they had been in the new house on the prairie for a year, Pa said they would have to leave. So once more Laura rode in the covered wagon, with Pa and Ma, Mary, and a new baby sister, Carrie. They returned to where they had started, the little house in the Big Woods of Wisconsin.

The days were full of work. Pa went far into the woods to hunt for meat and trap for furs. Ma was always busy, and Mary and Laura helped to churn butter, sew quilts, wash dishes, and sweep the log floor. Laura's special job was to bring in chips from the woodpile. She filled her apron full, for the fire on the hearth must never burn out. At night Pa played his fiddle, and music filled the little house from the pantry to the attic. Sometimes wolves howled outside, but Laura knew that Pa and Jack would keep them all safe.

As Laura grew older, more and more settlers crowded into the Big Woods. Pa wanted to be where neighbors were not so close and wild animals roamed free. So on Laura's seventh birthday, Mary, Laura, and Carrie were once again bundled inside the covered wagon. As they drove away, they saw their little log house for the last time. They headed west, to the wide, open prairies of Minnesota.

Pa found a new farm along Plum Creek, near the little town of Walnut Grove. At first they lived in a tiny one-room house that was hollowed into the bank of the creek. Its roof was made of sod, the same thick tangled grass that grew on the prairie. The dugout was cool in the summer and snug in winter, and the Ingallses lived in it until Pa built a wonderful new house made of sawn lumber. Nearby he grew a field of golden wheat.

Laura and Mary went to school in Walnut Grove. There Laura made new friends and learned to love reading and writing. Then one terrible day grasshoppers dropped from the sky, eating Pa's wheat crop and every other green growing thing. There was no crop for Pa to sell, so Pa had to go far away to find work. Laura and Mary helped with the chores on the farm, and Ma taught the girls their lessons at home. The girls could not walk to school anymore because the ground was covered with grasshoppers. They were all very busy, but still the weeks and months without Pa were long and lonely.

Pa finally came home, but he was restless in grasshopper country. Laura was not surprised when Pa told them they were going to move again. This time they were going to go to the town of Burr Oak, Iowa, to help run a hotel.

The Burr Oak hotel was a bustling place, with people coming and going, and covered wagons parked in the yard each night. When they were not in school, Laura and Mary helped in the kitchen and washed piles of dishes. Laura also took the cow to the pasture in the morning and brought her back home at night, and often she ran errands for the hotel's guests. One day when Laura returned home, she found she had a brand-new baby sister! Pa and Ma named the baby Grace.

Laura and her family were busy in Burr Oak, but they all missed the prairie country. So after two years they left Burr Oak and returned to Walnut Grove. Then Pa traveled far away by

covered wagon to begin a job as storekeeper for the new railroad line that was being built to link Minnesota and Dakota Territory. Ma and the girls followed Pa by train.

Laura was now twelve, and she had a special duty. During a long sickness Mary had become blind, and Pa asked Laura to become Mary's eyes. So all the way to Dakota Territory Laura told Mary about the train's smoking engine and about the people who sat on the plush red-velvet seats in the train car. When the family was settled in the railroad camp, Laura told Mary about the railroad men and their strong horses, busily working to build the track across the rolling prairie.

During their first winter in Dakota territory, Laura's family had almost no neighbors. But in the spring farmers crowded onto the land, and the town of De Smet sprang up overnight. Laura and Pa missed the empty prairie, but the Ingalls family would move no more. Pa had promised Ma that they would stay in De Smet so the girls could go to school. During the summer the family lived on their homestead, but in the winter they lived in town so Laura and Carrie could walk to school. At night Laura repeated her lessons to Mary so Mary could keep up with her studies, too. Mary wanted to go to the College for the Blind in Iowa, and Laura wanted to help her in any way she could.

The winters in Dakota Territory were fierce, and sometimes Laura and Carrie could not walk to the schoolhouse because of the snow. One winter the blizzards were so severe that the trains stopped running, and the stores ran out of food and fuel. For months Laura's family huddled together in their town building. Laura twisted hay to burn and ground wheat for flour until her hands ached. Everyone might have starved, but two boys, Almanzo Wilder and Cap Garland, made a dangerous trip across the frozen prairie to bring food back to the hungry townspeople.

When Laura was fifteen, she became a teacher in a tiny school twelve miles from De Smet. There were just five students, and two were almost Laura's age, but Laura was a good teacher. She lived with a family near the school and was very lonely for Pa and Ma and her sisters. She did not expect to see her family for the two months she would be teaching. But as her first week of teaching ended, Almanzo Wilder came with his sleigh and fast horses to take Laura home. Each Friday Almanzo drove Laura home, and each Sunday he brought her back to school. Laura loved skimming across snowy prairie behind Almanzo's beautiful brown

horses. And when school ended, she had earned forty dollars to help pay Mary's expenses at the College for the Blind.

When Laura returned to De Smet, Almanzo still took her on sleigh rides. And in the spring he took her for rides in his shiny black buggy. They rode to singing school, to church parties, to ice-cream socials, and to see Almanzo's homestead claim. They went to the nearby lakes, where they picked prairie roses and wild grapes and listened to the waves lapping against the shore. On one of their rides, Almanzo asked Laura to marry him, and she said yes.

In 1885, when Laura was eighteen, she and Almanzo were married and went to live in their own little gray house on the prairie. Laura was no longer a pioneer girl. She was now a homesteader's wife, and she soon learned to cook and bake and clean as well as Ma. But Laura still loved to be outdoors on the prairie. She and Almanzo galloped across the prairie on their horses to visit Pa and Ma, or to watch a glorious sunset. And the second winter they were married, Laura and Almanzo had their own daughter. They named her Rose, for those sweet-smelling blossoms that covered the prairies in summer.

After Rose was born, sad times came to the Wilders. First the crops dried up in the hot weather. Then Almanzo and Laura became ill. After they recovered, Almanzo could not use his right leg very well. Far worse, Laura and Almanzo's second child, a boy, died soon after he was born. Then one terrible day the little gray house burned down. These were unhappy days for Laura, but she was a pioneer and she knew she was tougher than hard times.

Hoping to make a fresh start, Laura, Almanzo, and Rose left the prairie and traveled south by train to Florida. They thought that the warmer weather would make Almanzo stronger, but the scrubby pine trees, sandy soil, and hot summer made the Wilders homesick. They returned to De Smet, still planning to start a new farm and build another home someday. Laura sewed for a dollar a day, and Almanzo worked at any job he could. Rose was now five, and she began school.

One day a friend gave Laura the biggest, reddest apple she had ever seen. It came from Missouri, the Land of the Big Red Apple. Laura and Almanzo learned that there was rich farmland for sale in Missouri. In 1894 they decided to move to Missouri and buy a farm with the one hundred dollars that Laura had been able to save from her sewing job. Just as Ma and Pa had done, Laura and Almanzo packed up all their belongings in a covered wagon to move to a new land.

Laura kept a diary of the forty-five days it took the family to travel from De Smet to Missouri. She wrote of the hot, dusty miles, the water-starved prairie farms they passed, and finally of Missouri's rolling green hills, apple orchards, and rushing creeks. As they drove into a town in the Ozark Mountains called Mansfield, Laura told Almanzo and Rose, "This is where we stop." They bought a hilly, tree-covered farm a mile from Mansfield, and Laura named it Rocky Ridge Farm. The Wilders moved into a tiny one-room log cabin that stood under tall trees and reminded Laura of her first home in the Big Woods of Wisconsin. With Rose's help, Laura cleaned the cabin and made it cozy for the coming winter, while Almanzo began clearing the land. The Wilders were finally home.

Laura and Almanzo worked together to make their new land a farm. They cut down trees, cleared away stones, and planted an apple orchard. While waiting for their land to grow good crops, Laura, Almanzo, and Rose moved to the town of Mansfield. Their house was close to Mansfield's first school, and Rose quickly became one of the school's best readers, spellers, and writers, as Laura had always been. To earn money, Almanzo delivered oil and stove gas in a horse-drawn delivery wagon, and Laura cooked meals for railroad workers. Laura soon became known in Mansfield as a good cook, a hard worker, and a cheerful neighbor. She shared with the community her good ideas, such as holding the town's first church bazaar. Mansfield people were glad that the Wilder family had come to their town.

Before they moved back to Rocky Ridge Farm, Laura and Almanzo built a new house on their land, using their own trees for lumber. When the house was finished, it had ten rooms, three porches, and thirty windows! When she cooked or sewed or worked inside, Laura could look out on the trees and curving hills of Rocky Ridge Farm.

Even as an adult Laura liked to be outside as much as she had when she was a pioneer girl. She waded in the creek, ran races up the hills with Rose, and hunted for berries in the woods. She tamed wild birds and small animals and had picnics with friends. In the evenings Laura, Almanzo, and Rose sat around the fireplace eating popcorn and apples, while Laura read aloud. She read books, newspapers, magazines, and letters from the family in De Smet. In these letters Laura learned that Mary, who had graduated from the College for the Blind, was living with Ma and Pa and helping with work at home and at church. Carrie was working at the De Smet newspaper office, and Grace had married a farmer who lived nearby. One day a letter came saying that Pa was very sick. Laura immediately traveled back to De Smet by train and was with him when he died.

Pa's pioneer spirit lived on in Laura and in Rose, too. Both Laura and Rose loved to travel to new places, and both of them were good storytellers. When Rose graduated from school, she became a journalist and traveled all over the world. She wrote books and stories about the places she visited, and she often sent home long letters about her adventures. Laura and Almanzo were proud that their Rose had become a famous writer.

In 1915, when Laura was forty-eight years old, she made her farthest trip west. She traveled to San Francisco, where Rose was living, to visit her daughter and see a world's fair. Almanzo stayed home to tend the farm, but Laura wrote him letters about the wonders she and Rose saw, like the Pacific Ocean and the giant redwood trees, and the fair exhibits.

After farming for thirty years, Laura and Almanzo decided to rest. They hired another farmer to raise their crops and look after their animals. Then, in their bright-blue car, they took trips near and far. On one trip they traveled back to De Smet, over the same roads they had traveled in their horse-drawn wagon so many years before. Ma and Mary had died, but Laura visited Carrie and Grace.

Laura was now past sixty, but she had never forgotten her days as a pioneer girl. She realized how much she missed those times with Pa and Ma and her three sisters in the Big Woods of Wisconsin and on the western prairies. So Laura decided to write down her memories of her childhood. She wrote whenever she had time, between cooking and working in the garden and going for drives with Almanzo. When she had finished, there were enough stories for her first book, *Little House in the Big Woods*. Laura wrote the book especially for children, so they could know how the pioneers had lived. Children liked this book so much that Laura wrote a second one, called *Farmer Boy*, all about Almanzo's life on a farm in northern New York when he was a boy.

In houses and schools and libraries all over America, and then all over the world, children, parents, and teachers alike loved Laura's stories. They sent her letters begging her to write more. For eleven years Laura worked on the books that came to be known as the Little House series. In them she told the story of her life, from her childhood in the Big Woods through her early years with Almanzo on the Dakota prairie. To her great surprise, Laura's Little House books made her a famous author. She was invited to speak at schools and on the radio, her books received awards and honors, and many libraries were named in her honor. From everywhere children sent her letters, presents, and drawings, thanking her for her stories. Many people even traveled to Mansfield, hoping to meet Laura or just see where she lived.

Laura was delighted that her books were loved by so many. And she was glad that through her stories, children could learn something of the pioneer days of America. But when she was seventy-six, Laura decided to write no more. Instead, she and Almanzo kept busy on their farm. They went for drives, visited friends, played games, and listened to the radio.

In 1949 Almanzo died at the age of ninety-two. Laura stayed on Rocky Ridge Farm, where there were so many memories of happy times. Although Laura lived alone until her death in 1957 at the age of ninety, she was never lonely. Friends came to visit almost every day. Once Laura invited the entire fourth-grade class from the Mansfield school to the farmhouse for a party. She told the children stories and let them roam through the big old house. The children ate cookies Laura had baked and enjoyed themselves. One boy told Laura he would rather read her Little House books than eat!

"I'm glad if my books have helped the children," Laura said when people praised her stories. She was pleased that she had done what she had set out to do: to tell the tales of the American pioneers for children everywhere and always.